Math on the Job

Math on the Farm

Tracey Steffora

Heinemann
LIBRARY

Chicago, Illinois

Edited by Dan Nunn and Abby Colich
Designed by Victoria Allen
Picture research by Tracy Cummins
Production control by Vicki Fitzgerald

Printed and bound in China by Leo Paper Group

15 14 13 12
10 9 8 7 6 5 4 3 2 1

Library of Congress Cataloging-in-Publication Data
Steffora, Tracey.
  Math on the farm / Tracey Steffora.—1st ed.
      p. cm.—(Math on the job)
  Includes bibliographical references and index.
  ISBN 978-1-4329-7156-4 (hb)—ISBN 978-1-4329-7163-2 (pb)
1. Farms—Juvenile literature. 2. Farm life—Juvenile literature. 3.
Mathematics—Juvenile literature. I. Title.

S519.S74 2013
630—dc23   2012013381

Acknowledgments
The author and publishers are grateful to the following for
permission to reproduce copyright material: Corbis: pp. 8
(© Ian Lishman/Juice Images), 12 (© Juice Images); Getty
Images: pp. 10 (Cultura/Monty Rakusen), 11 (Simon Rawles),
14 (Dr. Marli Miller); iStockphoto: pp. 7 (© Dan Moore),
19 (© emholk), 21 (© Gord Horne), 23a (© Gord Horne);
Shutterstock: pp. 4 (Noam Armonn), 5 (Goodluz), 6 (Denis
and Yulia Pogostins), 9 (Burry van den Brink), 13 (picsbyst),
15 (Vladislav Gajic), 16 (Gemenacom), 17 (Deymos),
20 (Denis and Yulia Pogostins), 23b (Denis and Yulia
Pogostins); Superstock: p. 18 (© imagebroker.net).

Front cover photograph of a man feeding chickens
outdoors reproduced with permission from Getty Images
(Johnny Valley).

Back cover photograph of a hand holding seeds
reproduced with permission from Shutterstock.com
(Denis and Yulia Pogostins).

Every effort has been made to contact copyright holders of
any material reproduced in this book. Any omissions
will be rectified in subsequent printings if notice is given to
the publisher.

Contents

Math on the Farm

Plants grow on a farm.

Animals live on a farm.

A farmer works on a farm.

A farmer uses math.

Counting

The farmer counts seeds.

The farmer counts eggs.

The farmer counts animals.

How many cows can you count?

(answer on page 22)

Measuring

scale

The farmer measures how heavy.

crop

The farmer measures how much.

The farmer measures how long.

There are shapes in the water.

This hay makes a rectangle.

What shape does this hay make?

(answer on page 22)

Time

The farmer knows what time to water the plants.

The farmer knows what time
to feed the animals.

The farmer plants seeds in the spring.

The farmer harvests the plants.

What season is this?

(answer on page 22)

Answers

page 9: There are three cows.

page 13: The dark horse is taller than the light brown horse.

page 17: The hay makes circles.

page 21: The season is fall.

Picture Glossary

harvest to pick and gather plants when they are ready

seed small plant part that can grow into a new plant

Index

Notes for parents and teachers
Math is a way that we make sense of the world around us. For the young child, this includes recognizing similarities and differences, classifying objects, recognizing shapes and patterns, developing number sense, and using simple measurement skills.

Before reading
Connect with what children know.
Ask children to name some things they have recently eaten, and discuss how those items, and most of our food, came from a farm. Talk about the work that people do on farms, working with plants and animals. Encourage children to discuss any experience they have had visiting a farm or learning about the plants and animals that grow on farms.

After reading
Build upon children's curiosity and desire to explore.
Revisit the picture on page 7 of a farmer counting eggs. Ask children if they know how we usually buy eggs in a store (in a carton of one dozen eggs). Explain that a dozen is another name for 12. Have an empty egg carton available and allow children to practice counting 12 objects into the spaces of the carton.

Discuss how time and seasons are very important to the job of the farmer. Review the four seasons and talk about how plants and animals grow around the seasons. Collect photos that show farms across the seasons and have children sort the photos by season.